A ROMAN RESCUE

To Conrad and Imogen, with all my love, E.D.
For Lauren and Marcus with love, K.A.G.

A TEMPLAR BOOK
First published in the UK in 2011 by Templar Publishing,
an imprint of The Templar Company Limited,
The Granary, North Street, Dorking, Surrey, RH4 1DN
www.templarco.co.uk

Text copyright © 2011 by Kelly Gerrard
Illustration copyright © 2011 by Emma Dodd

First edition

ISBN 978-1-84877-191-8

Edited by Libby Hamilton

Printed in Hong Kong

A CHARLIE AND BANDIT ADVENTURE

A ROMAN RESCUE

ADVENTURE BY

K.A. GERRARD

DRAWN BY

EMMA DODD

templar publishing

You'll stay locked up from now on. We wouldn't want anything to happen to you. I've got big plans for you, Bandit. Very big plans...

Where are you, Bandit? I miss you... I miss everyone.

BRUTUS AND SON
BUTCHERS SINCE AD43

CHARIOT
RACE
CIRCUS
MAXIMUS

Hello, I see you're a fan of the races?

Chicken or beef?

Actually, I've got an offer for you...

BUTC

Charlie's

NOTEBOOK

Useful things to remember
if you're ever in
ancient Rome

THE ROMAN EMPIRE

When I landed in ancient Rome, it was the time of the Roman Empire, which lasted about 500 years. It was governed by an emperor and a bunch of men like Cosmo's dad, called senators. Hadrian was the emperor when I was there.

I didn't like him much, but he ordered Hadrian's Wall to be built in northern England, which is over 115 kilometres long You can still see it today, so I guess he knew what he was doing.

GODS and GODDESSES

The Romans had hundreds of different gods and goddesses, like Minerva, the goddess of war, and Apollo, the god of music. Sadly, there wasn't a god of skateboarding.

Jupiter was the king of the gods and ruled the sky with his thunderbolt. The Romans built huge temples to their gods and sacrificed food and live animals. Porcus tried to sacrifice Bandit to Fortuna because she was the goddess of luck. Luckily we stopped that!

Charlie Tucker — skateboard GOD!

THE COLOSSEUM

Cosmo showed me the Colosseum - it was massive, fitting over 50,000 people! He called it an amphitheatre and, just like our theatres, people went there to watch shows. But he said most of their shows were pretty gory - gladiators or huge wild animals fighting each other. Not your typical panto!

THE CIRCUS MAXIMUS

This was the biggest racetrack in the Roman Empire, with enough room for 250,000 spectators. Charioteers had to race around the track seven times — metal dolphins in the middle were used to count the laps — and the finish line was in front of the Imperial box. Forget the Grand National or Formula 1 — I'd definitely rather go back there.

CLOTHES

The first thing I noticed in ancient Rome was that men wore dresses. Even worse, to fit in I had to wear one too! Most people dressed in simple tunics, but rich men wore togas and rich women wore stolas.

JEWELLERY

They may have liked to wear dresses, but Roman men didn't wear lots of jewellery. Most just wore a ring. The ring Cosmo's dad wore showed that he was a senator. Roman women loved to wear loads of bling, so I guess things haven't changed much!

TOYS

I saw children from wealthy families playing with toys I definitely recognised, like skipping ropes, kites, dolls and marbles. No other skateboards though.

FOOD

At dinner in Cosmo's house, no one sat down — they lay on couches! Weird. I recognised almost all of the food they ate — figs, apples, bread, fish, meat and much more. But don't try asking for chips or chocolate — the Roman Empire had no potatoes or cocoa beans to make them with!

SCHOOL WORK

Children of really wealthy families like Cosmo's were taught at home by a tutor. Some parents sent their children to school. (Girls only went until they were 11 years old.) But most families were too poor — their children worked instead of going to school.

Porcus.
Oink, Oink!

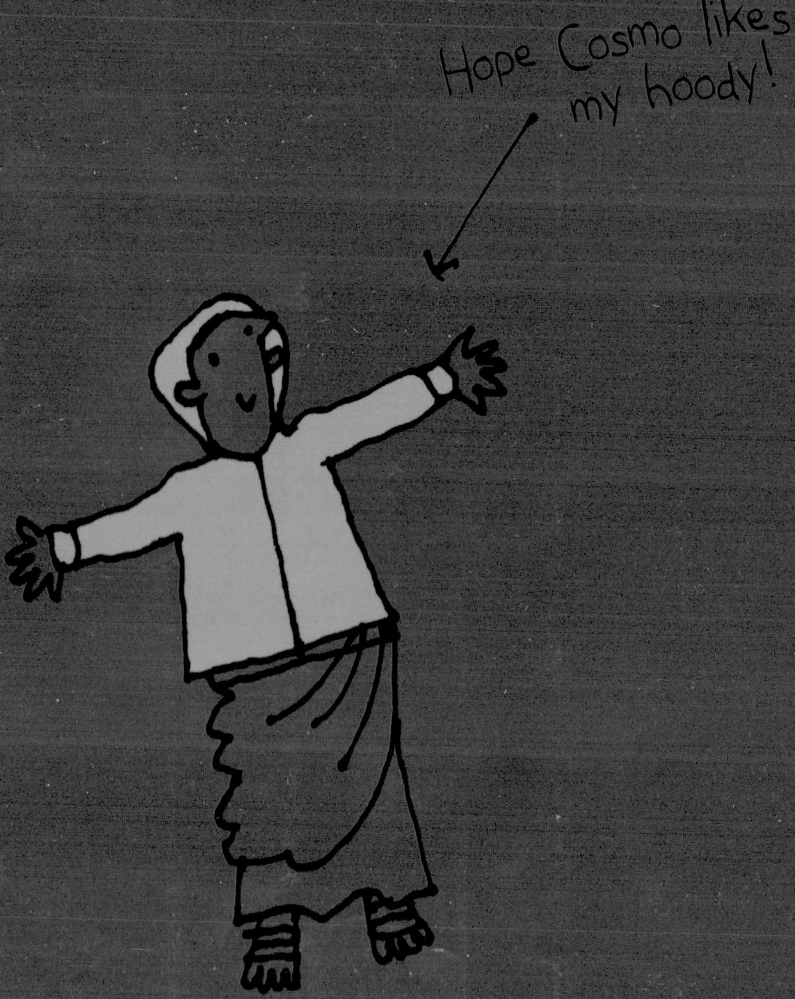
Hope Cosmo likes my hoody!